W9-AYB-913

ぼくらの運勢
Level 1
Just My Luck

IT'S TERRIBLY UNFORTUNATE TO BE BORN WITH BAD LUCK.
FOR EXAMPLE...
CRASH
...EEP!
...THIS SORT OF THING HAPPENING BECOMES A COMMON OCCURRENCE.

I, ASAHI NITTA, HAVE CONTINUED A LIFE LIKE THIS SINCE I CAN REMEMBER.
NOT THAT THIS IS NEW, BUT IT'S STILL BAD ON MY HEART...
AND THUS...
...I'VE COME TO RELY HEAVILY ON GOD, BUDDHA, AND EVEN DIVINATION. WHAT CAN I SAY? I'M HUMAN.
Divination Research Club
GOOD MORNING...
OH.
DID YOU HAVE ANOTHER TOUGH DAY?
AND...

YUP. LOOKS LIKE IT.
ぼ〜
...THE ONE PERSON I'VE COME TO RELY ON MOST...
YOU OKAY?
...IS THE ADVISOR FOR THE DIVINATION RESEARCH CLUB, ROKUJOU-SENSEI.
JUST THE SAME AS ALWAYS.

I'M FINE.
!
FINE?
ARE YOU SURE YOU DON'T NEED MY HELP?

NOW, THEN.
YOU HAVE TO ASK ME PROPERLY.
URGH.
SE...
"SENSEI..."
"PLEASE ..."
"...DO IT."
WELL DONE.

THIS IS MY "PURIFICATION RITUAL."
STRANGELY ENOUGH, ONCE I AM "PURIFIED," I'M OKAY FOR THE REST OF THE DAY.
AAH! ENOUGH OF THIS!
DO I HAVE TO KEEP SAYING THAT STUPID LINE?!
YES!
OR ELSE I CAN'T GET IN THE MOOD.
HE'S SORT OF A STRANGE GUY, BUT...
......

...HE'S AN EXPERT WHEN IT COMES TO ANCIENT DIVINATIONS FROM ALL OVER THE WORLD.
BESIDES, I CAN'T DENY HIS PREDICTIONS ARE USUALLY SPOT-ON.
I'M THE CHIEF OF THE DIVINATION RESEARCH CLUB, WITH HIM AS THE ADVISOR.
EVEN THOUGH I'M CURRENTLY THE ONLY MEMBER...
Club Orientation Meeting

WELL, WHAT DO YOU EXPECT? IT'S A PRETTY DAMN STRANGE CLUB TO BE IN.
YOU THINK SO? SEEMS LIKE A CLUB GIRLS WOULD WANT TO JOIN...
NO WAY!
THE STRANGEST THING ABOUT THE CLUB IS THE ADVISOR!
RIGHT! I'VE HEARD THE RUMORS!
HEY!
IS IT TRUE HE USES BLACK MAGIC?
AND THAT THERE'S A PILE OF HUMAN BONES TO USE FOR FORTUNE-TELLING?
AND THAT HE'S ALWAYS BOILING SOMETHING IN A CREEPY CAULDRON?
WHA...?
HOLD IT, GUYS! I KNOW HE SEEMS STRANGE, BUT IT'S NOTHING **THAT** EXTREME!

THINK ABOUT IT.
SOMETHING'S UP WHEN A GROWN MAN STILL BELIEVES IN STUFF LIKE FORTUNE-TELLING, RIGHT?
QUIT MAKING FUN OF HIM!
HE'S HELPED TONS OF PEOPLE THANKS TO THAT!
IT'S MY MISFORTUNE TO HAVE BAD LUCK.
THAT'S WHY...

...SENSEI'S "PURIFYING KISSES" ARE MY SALVATION.
THEY MAKE ME... HAPPY.
on Research Club
SENSEI, WHAT ON EARTH ARE YOU DOING?!

JUST FINISHING THE PREPARATIONS FOR THE CLUB ORIENTATION MEETING.
THAT'S GONNA HAVE THEM RUNNING SCARED INSTEAD!
SENSEI, DO YOU HAVE ANY IDEA WHAT THEY'RE SAYING ABOUT Y--
YES, I KNOW.
......
TH-THEN, WHY...?

WELL, I DON'T PARTIC-ULARLY CARE IF THEY LIKE ME OR NOT.

IF THEY THINK THIS IS CREEPY, THAT'S THEIR RIGHT.

ぎゅ...

WH-WHY...

...DO YOU HAVE TO PUT IT THAT WAY?

ASAHI?

I...I THINK YOU'RE--

I THINK YOU'RE REALLY AMAZING, AND I WANT EVERYONE ELSE TO RECOGNIZE THAT ABOUT YOU, TOO!
HELP ME OUT A LITTLE, PLEASE!
......

BUT I WOULDN'T MIND IF...
...YOU WERE THE ONLY ONE WHO THOUGHT THAT WAY ABOUT ME.
THE INFORMATION SESSIONS ARE NOW TAKING PLACE IN THE CLUBROOMS.
WILL ALL FIRST-YEARS PLEASE...
NO ONE'S GOING TO SHOW UP ANYWAY...
AND AFTER I...
...SAID ALL THOSE HARSH THINGS TO SENSEI...
COME ON NOW!

LOOK.
WE'VE GOT SOME NEW CANDIDATES FOR THE CLUB.
...HUH?!
B-BUT, WHY--?
I CALLED THEM HERE.
I HELPED YOU OUT.
DIDN'T I?
......
Y-YES!

OH, ARE YOU THE HEAD OF THE CLUB? I'VE HAD BAD LUCK FOR A LONG TIME NOW...
...SO I'M REALLY INTERESTED IN FORTUNE-TELLING AND STUFF!
REALLY? WELL, THEN...
OH...!
...IT LOOKS LIKE YOU'RE IN THE SAME PICKLE AS THE CLUB CHIEF HIMSELF!
PERHAPS I COULD HELP PURIFY YOU.
REALLY?! OH, THAT'D BE WONDERFUL!
THE SAME...
...AS HE DOES WITH ME.

TO DO THE SAME THING ... ...WITH HER?
CHIEF?
UM...
GOOD LUCK WITH THE REST ON YOUR OWN!

ASAHI?!
WHY...?

WHY DID I RUN AWAY?
IT'S JUST...
...IMAGINING SENSEI KISSING THAT GIRL MADE ME...
SKUFF
THAT WON'T DO.
THE HEAD OF THE CLUB CAN'T DISAPPEAR ON THE JOB.

IT LOOKED LIKE YOU WERE GETTING ALONG JUST FINE, SENSEI.
BE-SIDES.
I...
......
...MAY NOT BE CUT OUT FOR THE POSITION AS CHIEF.
THAT GIRL WAS JUST THE SAME AS ME! WANTING TO KNOW MORE ABOUT DIVINATIONS TO HELP HERSELF OUT.
I KNOW THAT YOUR "PURIFICATIONS" WOULD HELP HER, BUT...

...I DON'T WANT THAT.
SENS--
YOU WOULDN'T LIKE IT ...
...IF I DID THIS WITH HER?

YEAH...
BUT I DON'T--
IF YOU DON'T KNOW...
...THEN LET ME READ YOUR FORTUNE.

I SEE... YOU'RE IN LOVE WITH ME. RIGHT?
HUH?!
N-NO WAY! ER...
BUT MY PREDICATIONS ARE ALWAYS RIGHT, AREN'T THEY?
WELL, YEAH. I GUESS...
ASAHI, LISTEN TO ME.

I ALSO ...
...LOVE YOU.
SENSEI ALWAYS...
...!
IS THAT ALSO...A FORTUNE READING?
...MAKES ME HAPPY.
I MAKE A POINT TO NEVER READ MY OWN FORTUNE.

THAT'S WHY THESE ARE MY TRUE FEELINGS.
SO, THEY ALREADY LEFT.
OH.
Went to check other clubs.
BUT RIGHT NOW...
...IS THE FIRST TIME I'VE FELT THIS HAPPY.
LOOKS LIKE IT'S JUST THE TWO OF US AGAIN.

SO YOU REALLY WERE INTERFERING WITH MY RECRUITING OF NEW MEMBERS... WEREN'T YOU?
WELL, YOU WERE SO DESPER-ATE...
...TO LET OTHERS INTO OUR FABULOUS LITTLE CLUB.
I DON'T MIND IT STAYING LIKE THIS JUST A LITTLE LONGER.

YOU'RE, UH...
...GIVING ME A LOT MORE PURIFICATIONS THAN USUAL TODAY.
HEH HEH. TRUE.
......
AND I'LL GIVE YOU EVEN MORE.
HUH?
AH...!
HEY, IS IT ALL RIGHT IF I...KISS YOU SOMEWHERE *ELSE?*
......
かあああああ
ああ

MAY I?
......
"SENSEI..."
"PLEASE... DO IT."
WELL DONE.
SLIP

AND HERE...
...!
SENSEI!
ZZZIP
AH!

N-NOT... THERE!
IF ONES LOVES ANOTHER ...
...IT'S ONLY NATURAL TO KISS HERE, TOO.
KISS
...!
AH!
MMPH!
AAHN!
SUCK
SUCK
NO...!
SUCK
SENSEI!
SUCK
SLURP
AAH!

AH! I'M...
...G-GOING TO CUM! LET GO!
SLURP
AH...!
GO AHEAD.
...!
AND ABOUT BEFORE...
OF COURSE I WAS GOING TO GIVE THAT GIRL A DIFFERENT TYPE OF PURIFICATION.
BECAUSE...

...THIS KIND OF PURIFICATION ONLY WORKS ON THE ONE YOU LOVE.
IT'S THE FEELINGS WITHIN THE KISS THAT GIVES THE PERSON BLESSING.
!
WAIT A SEC.
HAVE YOU BEEN TRICKING ME THIS WHOLE TIME?
MAYBE, MAYBE NOT.

Just My Luck★Level 1 End

I HAVE EXTRA-ORDINARILY BAD LUCK.
OH, YESTERDAY WAS ALL RIGHT.
NO CAR ACCIDENTS AND NO GETTING MUGGED!
THAT'S GOOD TO HEAR.
THAT'S WHY I BECAME VERY SUPERSTITIOUS AND JOINED THIS CLUB.
Divination Research Club
MY LUCK IS SO BAD THAT I EVEN WORRY THE CLUB ADVISOR (AND DIVINATION MANIAC) ROKUJOU-SENSEI...
IN THAT CASE...
...HOW ABOUT I GIVE YOU ANOTHER PURIFICATION TO IMPROVE YOUR LUCK TODAY?
...AND SO...

...ME AND THAT CLUB ADVISOR HAVE BECOME... LOVERS.
ぼくらの運勢
Just My Luck
Level 2

WHENEVER HE KISSES ME LIKE THIS, STRANGELY ENOUGH, MY LUCK COMPLETELY TURNS AROUND!
MM...
W-WAIT. SENSEI?
HM?
RUSTLE
ER, STOP!
I, UH...
I HAVE CLASS SOON!
AH!
YO!

......
ICHINOSE?
LONG TIME, NO SEE!
IS HE A FRIEND?
WHAT ARE YOU DOING HERE?
IS THAT ANY WAY TO GREET YOUR CHILDHOOD FRIEND?
I'LL BE WORKING HERE STARTING TODAY.
SO I THOUGHT I'D POP IN AND SAY HELLO.

OH!
IS THIS THE UNLUCKY KID YOU WERE TELLING ME ABOUT BEFORE?
YUP.
HE'S THE HEAD OF THE CLUB--ASAHI.
HMM...
SO, ASAHI-KUN, IS IT?
NICE TO MEETCHA!
ER, PLEASED TO MEET YOU TOO, ICHINOSE... SENSEI.
I'VE REALLY ...

...BEEN LOOKING FORWARD TO MEETING YOU.
?
Laters!
BOY, HE REALLY IS A CHEERFUL AND FRIENDLY TEACHER!
HUH?
WELL, I WOULDN'T EXACTLY SAY HE'S A BAD GUY OR ANYTHING...
...BUT...

...HE HAS TIMES WHEN HE'S A BIT TOO MUCH.
IF I SAW YOU FOR THE FIRST TIME, I'D THINK *YOU* WERE BAD NEWS.
WATCH YOUR TONGUE, ASAHI.
BUT I SUPPOSE ...
...I MIGHT REALLY BE A BAD GUY.
OH!
AFTER ALL, I DO ALL THESE HORRIBLE THINGS TO YOU.
AH!
AH...!

I HAVE TO... GET TO CLASS!
AAH!
FOR HAVING SUCH BAD LUCK, I'M LUCKY ENOUGH TO HAVE SENSEI LOVE ME.
YOU'RE SO ADORABLE, ASAHI.
AH!
AAH!
...!

は…
AND YET, I'M STILL WORRIED.
UH...
AFTER ALL...
WH-WHAT ABOUT YOU, SENSEI?
に
IF YOU LEAVE NOW, YOU'LL MAKE IT IN TIME FOR CLASS.
YOU MAY GO NOW.

......
...SENSEI DOESN'T...
...ASK ANYTHING OF ME.
IT FEELS WRONG ALWAYS BEING THE ONLY ONE ALLOWED RELEASE.
BUT...
...I DON'T THINK I COULD EVER TELL HIM THAT.

MAYBE HE'S ONLY GOING OUT WITH ME...
...OUT OF PITY.
I'M SUCH A COWARD.
OOOH, YEAH. SHOW ME THAT CRESTFALLEN FACE!
ICHINOSE-SENSEI?
...?
UH, IF YOU'RE LOOKING FOR ROKUJOU-SENSEI, HE SHOULD BE IN THE PREPARATION ROOM.
NAH, I'M NOT HERE TO SEE HIM.

DIDN'T I TELL YOU BEFORE?
YOU'RE THE ONE I'VE BEEN DYING TO MEET.
HUH--?
!
HUH?!
WHY ...
...IS THIS HAPPEN-ING?

WHAT AM I...DOING IN HERE?
OH. THAT'S RIGHT.
ICHI-NOSE-SENSEI...
...KIDNAPPED ME!
But of course, no one noticed me getting kidnapped right on school grounds.
HEY THERE.
SO, YOU'RE AWAKE?
OH...

SORRY FOR BEING SO ROUGH WITH YOU.
BUT THIS IS FOR THE SAKE OF MY RESEARCH!
R-RESEARCH?
YOU SEE, YOU ARE VITAL TO THE SUCCESS OF MY RESEARCH!
DO YOU KNOW WHAT ENTROPY IS?
PRECISELY!
IT'S THE THEORY THAT ALL ENERGY IN THE UNIVERSE IS CONSTANTLY STRIVING TO REGAIN BALANCE WHEN OUT OF BALANCE!
AND IT'S MY RESEARCH THAT STATES THAT THIS CAN BE APPLIED TO HUMAN LUCK, AS WELL!

THUS, I BELIEVE YOU HAVE AN ENORMOUS AMOUNT OF GOOD LUCK COMING AFTER ALL THAT BAD LUCK YOU'VE HAD THUS FAR!
WHAT?!
AND I'D LIKE YOU TO ALLOW ME TO SURVEY THAT SITUATION...
...FOR THE REST OF YOUR LIFE.
WHA...?!
WHAT'S HE SAYING?!
OH! AND ONE MORE THING...
YOU...
...LOVE ROKUJOU, DON'T YOU?

HUH ...?
YOU WERE KISSING HIM THIS MORNING, REMEMBER?
HMM.
YOU MEAN, HE SAW US?!
IN THAT CASE...
MAYBE I SHOULD TRY THIS.
WH-WHAT ARE YOU GOING TO--
YOU WOULDN'T LIKE KISSING SOMEONE YOU DON'T LOVE, RIGHT?
......!

THE MORE UNLUCKY YOU BECOME, THE EASIER MY RESEARCH SHOULD GO.
THEN THIS SHOULD WORK JUST FINE.
...OH!
ROKUJOU-SENSEI!
HELP... ME!
HERE I AM...
...RELYING ON ROKUJOU-SENSEI AGAIN.
I JUST KEEP MAKING HIM WORRY!

BUT...
BUT...!
ROKU...
FOR HAVING JUST STARTED HERE, YOU'RE GETTING AWFULLY AHEAD OF YOURSELF.
ICHINOSE.

ROKUJOU...
MY FORTUNE-TELLING TOLD ME SOMETHING BAD WAS COMING, SO I CAME TO INVESTIGATE.
WHAT DO YOU MEAN "AWFULLY AHEAD"? WHAT'S THE BIG DEAL?
YOU'RE DOING THE SAME GODDAMN THING!
STAYING BY HIS SIDE AND WAITING FOR A FLOOD OF GOOD LUCK!
THAT WAS YOUR GOAL TOO, WASN'T IT?
ROKUJOU-SENSEI?
....

YOU THINK I'M GOING TO JUST SIT BACK AND ALLOW YOU TO USE ASAHI FOR YOUR SILLY RESEARCH?
DO YOU WANT ME TO...
...PUT A CURSE ON YOU THAT BADLY?
EEP!
ASAHI.
ARE YOU ALL RIGHT?

SENSEI...!
CAN YOU REALLY PUT CURSES ON PEOPLE, SENSEI?
EVEN IF I COULD, I WOULDN'T.
I SEE.
I THOUGHT YOU WERE REALLY GOING TO DO IT.
DIVINATION SHOULD ONLY BE USED TO GUIDE PEOPLE DOWN THE RIGHT PATH.
......
Phew!

I WAS SO SCARED.
AND YOU'D GOTTEN SO ANGRY...
DID ICHINOSE ...
...DO ANYTHING TO YOU?
DID HE KISS YOU?
OR DO SOMETHING ELSE?
SEN--
YOU'RE JUST SO...

...PRECIOUS TO ME.
I CAN'T...
...KEEP BEING A COWARD BECAUSE OF MY BAD LUCK.
I NEED TO....
SENSEI.
THEN, WOULD YOU...
...GO WITH ME... TO THE END?

I LOVE YOU!
BUT I... I'M ALWAYS THE ONLY ONE WHO...
ASAHI.
LISTEN.

DESPITE WHAT YOU SAY...
...I'M STILL AWARE THAT I'M A BAD ADULT.
A BAD ADULT WHO KEEPS TAKING ADVANTAGE OF YOU, EVEN WHEN YOU COME TO RELY ON ME.
THAT'S WHY I WANTED TO HOLD BACK A LITTLE LONGER, BUT...
NO...!
YOU'RE JUST TOO CUTE.
YOU MAKE ME SO HAPPY, ASAHI.

NOW THAT I GOT TO HEAR YOUR TRUE FEELINGS.
BUT DON'T COME CRYING TO ME...
...IF IT HURTS.
SENSEI...

HA...!
YOU OKAY, ASAHI?
WE'VE ONLY JUST STARTED.
KISS

I'M... OKAY.
DO... WHATEVER YOU... WANT!

...!
...HA!
AAH!
AH!
AAH!
ASAHI!
ASAHI...!

...!
ARE YOU... OKAY?
...!
SURE MY BODY HURT, BUT...
...I WAS SURE THAT...
......
I... CAN TAKE IT...
...SENSEI WAS TAKING A LOT OF CARE WHEN MAKING LOVE TO ME.

OH YEAH...
...I WONDER IF WHAT ICHINOSE-SENSEI SAID WAS TRUE.
AN ENORMOUS AMOUNT OF GOOD LUCK...
IF THAT...

Just My Luck ★ Level 2 End

Just My Luck ★ Level 3
Divination Research Club
WITH MY BAD LUCK, I JOINED THIS CLUB HOPING FOR SOME SALVATION.
DAY AFTER DAY, WE RESEARCH FORTUNE-TELLING AND CHARMS THAT IMPROVE LUCK.
ASAHI?
WOULD YOU STOP CALLING ME "ROKUJOU-SENSEI" AND JUST GO BY MY FIRST NAME? IT'S "NORITO."
THE ADVISOR ROKUJOU-SENSEI AND MYSELF, THE CLUB CHIEF, MAKE UP THE TWO MEMBERS.
?
DO YOU THINK IT'LL IMPROVE MY LUCK IF I DO THAT TODAY?

ぼくらの運勢

Just My Luck

Level 3

IS IT SO
BAD A
REQUEST?

UP UNTIL NOW, I'VE REALLY HAD NOTHING BUT BAD LUCK.
W-WELL, I GUESS NOT.
THEN, WOULD YOU CALL ME THAT?
BUT... WE'RE STILL IN THE SCHOOL.

YOO-HOO!
AND PEOPLE KEEP POPPING IN LIKE THIS.
What is it this time?
Uh-oh. You're angry again.
THIS IS HOW SOMEONE AS UNLUCKY AS ME GOT TO MEET SENSEI.
IT'S A LITTLE EMBARRASSING TO SAY, BUT I THINK THAT'S THE BEST LUCK I'VE EVER HAD.
WELL...
...IT'S ALMOST TIME FOR CLASS, SO I'LL BE GOING.
OH, AAAAASAHI-KUUUUN.

C'MON, NO NEED TO BE SO COLD-HEARTED.
I SWEAR I'M NOT PLANNING ON DOING ANYTHING LIKE THAT TO YOU AGAIN!
BUT I GOTTA SAY, HE'S ALWAYS BEEN SCARY LIKE THAT.
HAS ROKUJOU-SENSEI ALWAYS BEEN LIKE THAT?
ICHINOSE-SENSEI, YOU SAID YOU WERE FRIENDS WITH ROKUJOU-SENSEI WHEN YOU WERE STILL KIDS, RIGHT?
YEAH, WHAT OF IT?
HUH?
I'M SURE *YOU'D* PROBABLY KNOW MORE ABOUT HIM THAN *I* DO, RIGHT?
I MEAN, I'D HEARD YOU TWO WERE CLOSE WHEN YOU WERE LITTLE AND LIVING IN THE SAME TOWN.
WHAT...?

I NEVER HEARD ANYTHING ABOUT THAT!
WHAT DO YOU MEAN BY THAT?!
I DON'T REMEMBER BEING CLOSE TO HIM BEFORE.
THEN, WHY?
I ONLY MOVED THERE SHORTLY AFTER.
WHY HASN'T SENSEI TOLD ME ANYTHING ABOUT THIS?!
ASAHI?

YOU'VE BARELY TOUCHED YOUR FOOD. IS ANYTHING THE MATTER?
OH...
SENSEI.
UMM...
YES?
WHY WOULD HE...
......

ER, NO.
NEVER MIND. IT'S NOTHING.
...KEEP IT A SECRET ALL THIS TIME?
HE MUST HAVE SOME SORT OF REASON.
ASAHI?
WHAT ARE YOU DO--
MOM!
WHY DON'T I REMEMBER WHAT HAPPENED IN THE PAST?
ASAHI...

WELL, YOU SEE...
...I TRIED NOT TO BRING IT UP BECAUSE IT SEEMED YOU'D ALREADY FORGOTTEN ABOUT IT.
BUT LONG AGO...
...THERE WAS A FIRE IN THE APARTMENT WE USED TO LIVE IN BEFORE WE MOVED HERE.
NO ONE WAS HURT, BUT...
...YOU SEEMED TO BE REALLY TRAUMATIZED BY IT, SO...
...I THOUGHT IT BEST NOT TO REMIND YOU ABOUT IT.

THEN...
...WAS THERE SOMEONE IN OUR NEIGHBORHOOD NAMED "ROKUJOU"?
HUH?!
NOW THAT YOU MENTION IT, YES. I RECALL THERE WAS A SHINTO PRIEST FAMILY BY THE NAME OF "ROKUJOU."
IF THAT'S ALL TRUE...

...THEN WHY WOULDN'T HE TELL ME ANYTHING ABOUT IT?!
OH!
Rokujou
303
I CAME TO SENSEI'S PLACE WITHOUT EVEN THINKING.
WHAT DO I DO NOW?
SHOULD I BRING IT UP TO HIM?

SENSEI MIGHT HAVE A REASON FOR WHAT HE DID.
I KNOW IT MIGHT BE RUDE FOR ME TO FORCE HIM TO ANSWER, BUT...
ASAHI...
IS SOMETHING THE MATTER?

OH...
ER...
WELL, UH...
I WAS HOPING... YOU COULD HELP ME WITH MY HOMEWORK!
I COULDN'T GET IT, SO...
....
OH. OKAY. WOULD YOU LIKE TO COME IN?
AND!

I MISSED YOU.
THAT'S ALSO TRUE.
I'M HAPPY TO HEAR THAT, ASAHI.
WAIT HERE A SECOND
I'LL PUT SOME TEA ON FOR US.
I CAN AT LEAST TRY TO SEE IF IT'S TRUE OR NOT FOR MYSELF...

OH...

EXCUSE ME.
WHAT DO YOU THINK YOU'RE DOING?
ER, N--
NOTHING! JUST... WANTED TO TAKE A LOOK.
YOU KNOW IT'S IMPOLITE TO GO LOOKING THROUGH SOMEONE ELSE'S BOOKSHELF.
...!
OH, Y-YEAH?!

SO YOU'RE SAYING IT'S **NOT** IMPOLITE TO KEEP THE PAST A SECRET FROM SOMEONE ELSE FOR SO LONG?!
...... HOW MUCH HAVE YOU REMEMBERED?
THAT WE... USED TO KNOW EACH OTHER, WAY BACK WHEN.
IS THAT ALL?
YOU MEAN THERE'S MORE?

......
IF...IF WE WERE TOGETHER BACK THEN...
...I'D BE HAPPY TO KNOW ABOUT THAT. SO WHY...?
......
BECAUSE...
...I WOULDN'T WANT YOU TO HATE ME.
NOT AFTER IT TOOK SO LONG TO GET YOU TO LIKE ME AGAIN.

IT'S TRUE THAT WE USED TO LIVE IN THE SAME TOWN.
I'M SURE YOU MUST UNDER-STAND, SEEING THE WAY I AM NOW.
BUT EVER SINCE I WAS YOUNG, I'VE ALWAYS BEEN GOOD AT FORTUNE-TELLING. EVERYONE AROUND ME WAS AFRAID OF ME FOR HAVING SUCH A STRANGE POWER.
BUT AMIDST ALL OF THEM...
...YOU WERE THE ONLY ONE WHO GOT CLOSE TO ME.

YOU WERE SO CUTE.
OH, YOU'RE STILL CUTE NOW.
WHY DID YOU HIDE THAT FROM ME?
THERE'S MORE TO THE STORY.
WE WERE CLOSE FRIENDS, BUT...
...THE NEIGHBORS WHO DIDN'T THINK HIGHLY OF ME, STARTED THINKING THE SAME ABOUT YOUR FAMILY, TOO.
I WAS SO ANGRY... I DECIDED TO PUT A CURSE ON THEM.

YOU TRIED TO STOP ME.
YOU COULD SENSE THAT I WAS GOING TO DO SOMETHING BAD.
NO, NORITO!
DON'T DO IT!
AFTER THAT, YOUR HOME CAUGHT ON FIRE.
THAT... CAN'T BE!
I THOUGHT THAT WHAT I'D DONE FELL ON YOU INSTEAD.
ASAHI.
THE REASON FOR YOUR BAD LUCK MIGHT HAVE BEEN BECAUSE OF WHAT I DID BACK THEN.

SO? DO YOU HATE ME NOW?
HOW CAN YOU SAY THAT?
BUT MY HOUSE...
EVERYONE GOT OUT ALL RIGHT.
AND BESIDES, I...

...THINK THE LUCKIEST THING THAT'S HAPPENED TO ME...
...WAS MEETING YOU, SENSEI.
I'VE ALWAYS FELT THAT WAY.
AND I'M SURE I ALWAYS WILL.

......
ASAHI...
WON'T YOU CALL ME "NORITO"?
Aah...
WE'RE NOT IN SCHOOL RIGHT NOW, ARE WE?
YOU USED TO CALL ME THAT, BACK THEN.
IT ALWAYS MADE ME FEEL SO CALM.
......

NORITO...
ASAHI...
......

THAT'S RIGHT.
I REMEMBER THIS SCENE.
A GENTLE FACE LOOKING DOWN AT ME.
ASAHI.
I LOVE YOU...

MMPH...
ASAHI.
I LOVE YOU, ASAHI.

SOMETHING ABOUT THE WAY HE SAYS THAT OVER AND OVER...
...HAD A FAMILIAR RING TO IT.

HEY.
YOU OKAY?
YEAH...
......

BY THE WAY...
...AFTER WE FINALLY MET AT THIS SCHOOL AGAIN...
...YOU SAID THE SAME THING YOU USED TO SAY WHEN YOU WERE A KID.
YOU MAY SEEM WEIRD, SENSEI...
...BUT I DON'T MIND IT AT ALL.
......
OF COURSE.

THAT'S BECAUSE I'VE ALWAYS LOVED YOU, NORITO.
BEING ABLE TO SEE YOU AGAIN...
...HAS TO BE THE GREATEST LUCK I'VE EVER HAD.
Just My Luck★Level 3 End

I USED TO LOVE THOSE SKILLED AND GENTLE HANDS.

恋する機械

Mechanism of Love

IT'S RARE FOR ME TO GET A VISITOR IN MY HOME, WHERE I LIVE DEEP IN THE MOUNTAINS.
AND TODAY I HAD TWO.
BIG BROTHER, I BROUGHT HIM BECAUSE I THOUGHT HE'D BE PERFECT FOR YOU.
MY YOUNGER SISTER...
IT'S NOT RARE THESE DAYS TO HAVE ONE.

...AND AN ANDROID THAT SHE DEVELOPED.
I MEAN, LIVING WITH AN ANDROID...
...IS PARTICULARLY COMMON AMONG THE ELDERLY--
AND LAST I CHECKED, I'M **NOT** ELDERLY.
BUT THAT'S WHY I'M WORRIED ABOUT YOU!
I MEAN, THE WAY YOU HATE PEOPLE SO MUCH, YOU'RE JUST LIKE AN OLD MAN HIDING AWAY IN THE MOUNTAINS!
IT'S NICE TO MEET YOU, MASTER.

DID HE JUST SAY, "MASTER"?
OH, I'VE ALREADY PROGRAMMED HIM TO RECOGNIZE YOU AS HIS MASTER.
NOW SEE IF HE CAN HELP YOU WITH YOUR PEOPLE-PHOBIA.
AND THAT'S HOW I GOT DUMPED...
...WITH "HIM."
I'LL DO MY BEST TO BE OF SERVICE TO YOU, MASTER.
....
LOOK, I DON'T HATE PEOPLE AS BADLY AS SHE PUT IT.

I'M JUST NOT GOOD AT DEALING WITH PEOPLE, AND SHE MAKES ME OUT TO BE SICK IN THE HEAD!
I UNDER-STAND, MASTER.
YOU'RE A VERY WONDERFUL PERSON.
WHA--?
WHAT ARE YOU SAYING?!
I'M SAYING, I DON'T SEE YOU AS SICK AT ALL.
YOU'RE SIMPLY...
...IN NEED OF REHABILITATION IN THE WAYS OF HUMAN AFFECTION.

ば
OH...
PLEASE.
DO NOT BE AFRAID.
THIS IS ONLY A FAKE HAND.
FAKE HAND?

HE'S RIGHT.
SEE?
Y-YES.
IT'LL BE A PLEASURE WORKING WITH YOU.
MASTER.
HE WAS MADE TO BE A SUBSTITUTION FOR FAMILY.
THE WAY HE ATE AND TOUCHED WAS COMPLETELY LIKE A HUMAN.
HOWEVER, ONCE A WEEK, HE'D NEED TO GO TO HIS MANUFACTURER (MY SISTER) FOR MAIN-TENANCE.

EVERY OTHER DAY, HOWEVER, HE WOULD HELP ME WITH MY WORK...
SO YOUR PROFESSION IS REPAIRING TOYS.
I'M NOT NEARLY AS SKILLED AS MY SISTER, SO THIS IS ALL I'M GOOD FOR.
YOU NEEDN'T SPEAK OF IT LIKE THAT. YOUR JOB IS ALSO WONDERFUL IN ITS OWN WAY.
...WHILE HELPING ME WITH MY REHABILI-TATION.
....
ぎゅ…

IT'S ONLY A FAKE...
...SO IT'S OKAY.
BUT HIS HANDS THAT TOUCHED ME WERE WARM AND GENTLE.
MASTER?
WHAT'S THIS?
DON'T TOUCH THAT!
...!

ER, I MEAN...
I...
I'M SORRY!
NOT AT ALL.
I AM THE ONE WHO SHOULD APOLOGIZE.
BUT...

I...
...LIKE THOSE KINDS OF MODELS.
......
AS AN ANDROID, YOU STILL HAVE LIKES AND DISLIKES?
......
I HAVE MANY ABILITIES.
THAT'S NOT FOR YOU TO SAY.
ぷ
BUT...
...I ALSO...

...LIKE MODELS LIKE THESE.
....

YOU... CARRIED ME?
HUH?
....
THANKS.
IT IS CLEAR...
...YOU ARE VERY PASSIONATE ABOUT YOUR WORK.

IT'S BECAUSE I WANT TO FIX THEM AS FAST AS I CAN.
THAT'S VERY KIND OF YOU.
...!
NO, IT'S CALLED WORK! IT HAS NOTHING TO DO WITH KI--
YOU REALLY ARE...
...VERY KIND, MASTER.
YEAH.
HE'S BEEN A GREAT HELP.

HE ALSO HELPS ME WITH MY WORK.
HE'S GOT SKILLED FINGERS.
YOUR HANDS ARE SO SKILLED, YOSHINO-KUN!
I LOVE THEM!
THEY'RE NOSTALGIC IN A WAY.
WELL, THAT'S GOOD TO HEAR.
HOW'S YOUR REHABILI-TATION COMING ALONG?
UH...

BEEP
IT'S GOING...
...JUST FINE.
WHAT WERE YOU TALKING ABOUT?
NOTHING. JUST TALKING SMACK ABOUT YOU.
WHAAT ?!
IT'S CALLED A JOKE.
YOU'VE GOT YOUR MAINTENANCE AGAIN TOMORROW.
GO TO MY SISTER'S.

"I'LL BE BACK THIS EVE-NING."
BOY, IT FEELS LIKE FOREVER...
...SINCE I WAS LAST ALONE.
I'M JUST NOT GOOD WITH PEOPLE...

I ALWAYS END UP HURTING SOMEONE.
"YOU REALLY ARE VERY KIND, MASTER."
....
THAT'S STRANGE...

I USED TO FEEL CALMER BEING ALONE.
DING DONG
HUH.
ANOTHER PACKAGE FOR WORK.
IT WASN'T...
...HIM?
は.
BUT THE PACKAGES USUALLY ARRIVE AROUND THIS TIME.
THE DELIVERYMAN DOESN'T EVEN WASTE HIS TIME CALLING ME TO THE DOOR.
...
BECAUSE I CAN'T STAND TO GO OUT-SIDE.
YET I...

DIDN'T HE SAY...
...HE'D BE BACK BY EVENING?
WHAT'S THE MATTER WITH ME NOW?
I'M BACK, MASTER!
......?
MASTER? WHAT'S THE MATTER? YOU DON'T LOOK WELL!
...I'M FINE.

NOW WON'T YOU HURRY UP AND TOUCH ME ALREADY?

ARE YOU WORRIED ABOUT THAT?

OH! FORGIVE ME.

I WAS SIMPLY WONDERING HOW LONG IT WILL TAKE YOU TO REPAIR IT.

I WON'T BE FIXING THAT ONE. IT'S NOT FOR WORK.

IT'S MINE.

ACTUALLY, IT BELONGED TO AN OLD FRIEND OF MINE.
AND I BROKE IT.
......
THEN PERHAPS IT IS BEST THAT YOU--
I CAN'T FIX IT JUST YET.
SEE...MY FRIEND AND I USED TO PLAY WITH THIS ALL THE TIME.
YOUR HANDS ARE SO SKILLED, YOSHINO-KUN!
I LOVE THEM!

YOU LOVE THEM?
YUP!
I LOVE YOUR HANDS, YOSHINO-KUN!
ぎゅ!
……
I...
I LOVE YOU.
GRIP
THOSE GENTLE AND SKILLED HANDS THAT I LOVED...
...QUICKLY TURNED INTO SOMETHING SCARY.

I KNOW IT WAS STUPID OF ME.
TO HURT HIM LIKE THAT.
I REALLY MESSED UP.
AND HIS VOICE WAS SO... SOFT BACK THEN.
YOUR HANDS REALLY...
...REMIND ME OF HIS.
WHAT WOULD YOU HAVE DONE IF YOU HAD NOT MESSED UP?

THERE MUST HAVE BEEN A REASON FOR WHAT YOU DID.
PERHAPS YOU SHOULD TRY SIMULATING WHAT HAPPENED.
?
IS THIS ANOTHER ONE OF YOUR REHABILI-TATIONS?
IT'S MY JOB.
....
YEAH. RIGHT.
THEN... OKAY. I GUESS.
CLACK

"I LOVE YOU."
ARE YOU ALL RIGHT?
YES...
I...
"I LOVE YOU, TOO."
"YOSHINO-KUN."
YOUR SKILLED AND GENTLE HANDS.

YOUR
GENTLE HANDS.

BUT THESE ARE FAKE HANDS.
I AM SURE... "HE" ALSO UNDER-STANDS.
WHERE DID HE...?

CLUNK
HUH?
A CELL PHONE?
But he's a robot.
......
W-WELL, I'M HIS MASTER, SO IT'S ALL RIGHT.
BEEP
YOU HAVE ONE NEW MESSAGE.
I'M SORRY FOR PUTTING YOU THROUGH ALL THIS TROUBLE FOR MY BROTHER.
IT'S MY SISTER'S VOICE!
BUT I CAN'T HAVE MY WORK DELAYED ANY LONGER!
COME BACK HERE AS SOON AS YOU CAN.
ガチャ.
MASTER?

SECTION CHIEF YOSHINO.
WHAT ...?
GIVE THAT BACK!
SHE SAID, SECTION CHIEF YOSHINO!
WAS SHE TALKING ABOUT *YOU?!*
THAT'S--
...!
......
YES. IT'S TRUE.
I'M YOUR CHILDHOOD FRIEND...
...YOSHINO.

B-BUT WHY WOULD YOU...?
I'M YOUR SISTER'S BOSS NOW.
WHEN I HEARD THAT SHE WAS RELATED TO YOU, I JUST ***HAD*** TO SEE YOU AGAIN!
I NEEDED TO... APOLOGIZE.
UNLESS I DID THIS, YOU'D HAVE NEVER--
THEN HIS HANDS...
...WERE NEVER FAKE TO BEGIN WITH!
SLAP
AH...
IT'S TRUE.
I WAS TRICKING YOU ALL ALONG.

SLAM
I'M SORRY.
BUT I JUST LOVED YOU SO MUCH.
WELL...
...HOW ELSE WAS I SUPPOSED TO REACT?!
IT FELT LIKE HE WAS JUST MAKING A FOOL OF ME. HIM AND MY SISTER.
NO. I'M JUST STILL AFRAID.

I HURT HIM.
HOW COULD I DO THAT...
...AGAIN?!
I AM SURE... "HE" ALSO UNDER-STANDS.
BUT, NOT THIS TIME.
I WON'T...

...MAKE THE SAME MISTAKE AGAIN!
I'LL FINALLY TELL THE REAL YOU...
...WHAT I HAVEN'T BEEN ABLE TO FOR ALL THESE YEARS.

I...I'M SORRY FOR HURTING YOU!
I'VE LOVED YOU ALL THIS TIME!

THEN I GOT BACK...
...THOSE GENTLE HANDS I LOVED SO DEARLY.

Mechanism of Love End

School
Uniforms
and
You

MY SCHOOL STILL USES TRADITIONAL GAKURAN FOR THE UNIFORMS. (TALK ABOUT ORTHODOX!)
WHEN I FIRST ENTERED, I THOUGHT ...
..."WELL, IT'S EASIER THAN WEARING CASUAL CLOTHES ALL THE TIME."
BUT NOW... MY GAKURAN HAS BECOME THE CAUSE OF MY GREATEST WORRY.
HEY THERE, SUGIURA-KUN!
WANNA EAT LUNCH TOGETHER?
WHY, YOU ASK?

Nurse's Office
IT'S BECAUSE THE SCHOOL NURSE, "GAKURAN FETISH" OGASAWARA KEEPS HANGING ALL OVER ME!
MY, MY, MY. YOU STILL LOOK THE BEST IN A GAKURAN IN THE ENTIRE SCHOOL.
I'VE ENDED UP SEEING HIM ALMOST EVERYDAY, BECAUSE I CAN'T TURN DOWN HIS PASSIONATE INVITES.
YOU REALLY LIKE THE SCHOOL UNIFORMS, DON'T YOU?
SIGH
AND NOW I'VE SOMEHOW BECOME HIS TEA BUDDY.

I'LL GIVE HIM ONE THING, THOUGH. HE'S GOOD AT HIS JOB.
I'M SO GLAD I GOT TO MEET SOMEONE LIKE YOU.
AND I'M SURE HE'S A GOOD GUY, BUT...THAT'S PART OF THE PROBLEM.
HM?
WHAT'S THE MATTER?
ER, UH--!
I-IT'S JUST THAT...
WELL, LOOK AT THAT!
SEE, HE'S WEARING THE EXACT SAME THING AS ME, ISN'T HE?!

SAME SCHOOL UNIFORM...
HECK, EVEN THE SAME HEIGHT!
HOW CAN YOU SAY THAT?!
NO, NO, NO! YOU TWO ARE **COMPLETELY** DIFFERENT!
WAAAAAAAH!
THOSE LONG AND SLENDER LIMBS...
THAT PALE NAPE PEEKING OUT FROM YOUR COLLAR...
THIS CHILDLIKE FACE...!
YOU'RE MY IDEAL STUDENT, WHO LOOKS GREAT IN A GAKURAN!
ぎゅー

IT'S JUST THE RIGHT SLIMNESS TO WEAR A GAKURAN.
?
...!
THESE HIPS, TOO...
WH-WHOA!
AAHN!
WHAT'S THE MATTER?
I CAN'T BELIEVE I JUST LET OUT A MOAN!
I'M SO EMBARRASSED!
ER, UH--!
L-LET GO OF ME!
SORRY, I JUST... GOT CAUGHT UP IN THE MOMENT.
OH...
LOOK GOOD IN A GAKURAN, RIGHT?
BUT YOU REALLY DO...
Sheesh! I'm sick of hearing that!

YES, INDEED.

JUST PERFECT IN IT.

I KNOW HE DOESN'T MEAN ANY HARM BY IT.

UH, WELL...

...I HAVE TO GET TO CLASS NOW.

AAHN!
......
IT LOOKS LIKE I'M REALLY THE ONLY STUDENT OGASAWARA TREATS THIS WAY.
AND AS PROOF OF THAT...
REALLY, SUGIURA.
YOU AND OGASAWARA ARE AWFULLY CLOSE, HUH?

...NO OTHER STUDENT IS AWARE OF HIS GAKURAN FETISH.
YOU ALWAYS EAT LUNCH TOGETHER, RIGHT?
MAYBE I SHOULD COME ALONG, TOO, SOMEDAY.
UH...
Y-YEAH. SURE. I'LL ASK HIM SOMETIME.
ALL THE STUDENTS SEEM TO LIKE HIM WELL ENOUGH.
IN THE NURSE'S OFFICE, HE'S GOT A WHOLE WARDROBE FULL OF UNIFORMS THAT HE CLAIMS ARE FOR WHEN STUDENTS "NEED TO GET CHANGED."
EVEN THOUGH HE'S AN ODDBALL.
HEY, LOOK!
IT'S OGASA-WARA!

I'M THE ONLY ONE WHO KNOWS.
......
SO WHY DOES...
...THAT FACT MAKE ME HAPPY?
本
OH...

School Uniforms of Interest
IT'S OGASA-WARA.
AND HE'S READING A BOOK ON SCHOOL UNIFORMS!
Pfft! Even on his days off?
SENSEI!
SUGI... URA... KUN?
Ha ha ha!
I CAUGHT YOU LOOKING THROUGH ANOTHER SCHOOL UNIFORM CATA-LOGUE!
YOU MUST REALLY LIKE THEM!

......
?
UH...
YEAH...
I...
...HAVE TO GET GOING.
WHAT GIVES? HE'S ACTING SO STRANGE.
USUALLY, HE SAYS...
..."YOU LOOK GOOD IN THAT GAKU--"

OH!
I GET IT NOW.
IS SUGIURA IN?
IT WASN'T ME HE WAS SO INTERESTED IN AT ALL!
IT WAS MY... SCHOOL UNIFORM.

SORRY, BUT HE'S NOT HERE.
I LIKED THINKING...
...THAT HE LIKED ME.
YOU HAVEN'T BEEN HANGING AROUND OGASAWARA MUCH THESE DAYS.
EVERY-THING OKAY?
YEAH. JUST FINE.
WHY...

...DO I FEEL SO LET DOWN?
I KNOW I'M ACTING LIKE A TOTAL DUMBASS.
SO... STUPID.

I'D LIKE TO BORROW YOU FOR A MOMENT.
YOU'VE BEEN AVOIDING ME.
THERE'S SOMETHING I'VE BEEN WANTING TO TELL YOU FOR THE PAST FEW DAYS NOW.

DO YOU FIND MY ATTENTION TO BE...A NUISANCE?
......
IT WAS, SINCE THE START.
?
AFTER ALL, YOU ONLY LIKED MY SCHOOL UNIFORM... NOT ME.
WHAT-- ?!
I'M RIGHT, AREN'T I?!
THE OTHER DAY, WHEN I TALKED TO YOU IN MY NORMAL STREET CLOTHES, YOU WERE ACTING ALL WEIRD!
THAT MUST MEAN I'M ONLY GOOD FOR LOOKING AT WHEN IN MY SCHOOL UNIFORM!

SO JUST FORGET ABOUT IT! DON'T BOTHER ME ANYMORE!
YOU LOVE SCHOOL UNIFORMS, DON'T YOU, SENSEI?!
YES! I DO!
...
S-SEE--?
BUT...

I LOVE YOU, TOO!
THAT'S WHAT... I'VE BEEN WANTING TO TELL YOU.
I WAS JUST SO FLUSTERED THAT DAY.
TO BE HONEST, I THOUGHT I ONLY LIKED YOU AT FIRST BECAUSE YOU WERE WEARING THE SCHOOL UNIFORM.
BUT WHEN I SAW YOU IN NORMAL CLOTHES, MY HEART WAS ABOUT TO BURST. THAT'S WHEN I REALIZED.

I REALIZED THAT...
...I LOVE YOU.
YOU'RE LYING.
LIKE HELL, I AM.
DO YOU...
...LOVE ME, TOO?
......

"I LIKED THINKING THAT HE LIKED ME."
I...
...THINK I...
...DO.
SUGIURA-KUN...

KISS
LISTEN...
I WANT TO LOVE YOU... WITHOUT YOUR UNIFORM ON.
MAY I?
OGASAWARA MAY BE AN ODD TEACHER, BUT...
SUGIURA-KUN...
O-OH! SENSEI...! I...
I CAN'T!

ARE YOU SURE? YOUR BODY'S TELLING ME SOMETHING ELSE.
AH!
I LOVE YOU.
AH!
AAHN...
SEE? HE CAN EVEN SAY SUCH EMBARRASSING LINES SO EASILY!
DOES THIS TURN YOU ON?

BUT...
ぴちゃ…
は…
AAH!
AH...
AAH...
ぴちゃ…
FORGIVE ME.
I CAN'T HOLD BACK ANY LONGER!
...!

School Uniforms and You End

The Rumored Pair
HERE IN THIS ALL-DORM ALL-BOYS' MORIGAOKA HIGH SCHOOL...
...THERE ARE FEW WHO SELF-SUFFICIENTLY WALK DOWN A ROSE-STUDDED PATH.
I, HIROSHI AKABANE, VICE PRESIDENT OF THE STUDENT COUNCIL...
AOYAMA...
AKABANE...
...BEAR JUST THAT SORT OF FORBIDDEN LOVE TOGETHER WITH THE COUNCIL PRESIDENT, SEIICHI AOYAMA.

NOT!
HERE, WOULD YOU STAPLE THESE FOR ME?
Here, the legislative bill proposals.
YES, OF COURSE.
JUST WHY DO WE HAVE TO STAPLE THE BILLS BY OURSELVES?
The council president and vice-president shouldn't have to do these lowly jobs.
I WONDER IF THEY'RE TRYING TO GIVE US PRIVACY?
THOSE RUMORS SPREADING AROUND REALLY ARE A PAIN.
パチ
WE'RE HONESTLY THE MOST AVERAGE COUPLE OF FRIENDS YOU COULD FIND, BUT...
...EVERYONE AROUND US KEEPS SAYING, "YOU'D LOOK SO GOOD TOGETHER AS A COUPLE!"
WHAT, DO THEY THINK WE'RE GOING TO KISS OR SOMETHING WHEN WE'RE ALONE?
I LIKE GIRLS, YOU KNOW.
I've about had it.
YEAH, ME, TOO.

YUP, WE'RE JUST FRIENDS.
RIGHT?
I FEEL THE MOST AT EASE WHEN I'M WITH HIM.
?
HUH?
THE... MOST?

WH-WHAT DID I MEAN BY "MOST"?
IS HE REALLY THAT SPECIAL TO ME?
CLUNK
HEY, AKABANE?
WH- WHAT?
WEREN'T YOU LISTENING?
I WAS JUST SAYING HOW THE WAY THEY GO ON HOME BY THEMSELVES SHOWS HOW THEY REALLY DON'T KNOW WHAT TRUE FRIENDSHIP IS.
URK!

GOD-DAMN IT!
FOR A SECOND THERE, HE LOOKED REALLY FRICKIN' COOL!
HELLO?
Y-YEAH. RIGHT. FRIENDS.
CUZ WE'RE JUST FRIENDS!
SHEESH, WHAT'S GOTTEN INTO YOU?
SORRY.
THAT'S RIGHT.
HE'S JUST MY BEST FRIEND.
......
AKA-BANE?

HUH?
KISS
......
WH--
WHA--
WHA--
WHAT GIVES?!
MM, OH NOTHING.
IT'S JUST THAT CLOSE UP, YOU WERE ACTUALLY...

...PRETTY CUTE LOOKING.
I WANTED TO SEE WHAT IT'D BE LIKE TO KISS YOU, JUST LIKE EVERYBODY'S SAYING.
IT WAS JUST AN EXPERI-MENT.
WELL THEN QUIT EXPERI-MENTING ON ME!!
SORRY, BUT THINGS EAT AT ME UNLESS AS I EXAMINE THEM FURTHER.
WH-WHAT'S WITH THAT STUPID "EXPERI-MENT"?!
JUST LOOK WHAT IT DID TO ME!
MY HEART'S BEATING A MILE A MINUTE NOW--
WAIT A MINUTE. HUH...?

AM I SERIOUS ?!
COULD I ACTUALLY... LIKE HIM?!
B-BUT IF I DID, I'M SURE AOYAMA WOULDN'T LIKE THAT.
AND IT APPEARS THE RESULTS...
... SAY ...
...THAT I MAY NOT MIND IF EVERYONE CONTINUES THINKING WHAT THEY THINK ABOUT US.
WHAT?!
OFFICIALLY A COUPLE?
The Rumored Pair End

Hello, everyone. This is Temari Matsumoto.

This time, I'd like to thank you all for buying--no, READING-- *Just My Luck*.

And a special thanks goes out to Barugo-chan for always assisting me as usual

And also a huge heartfelt show of gratitude for my editor, A-sawa-sama, for looking out for me after all the trouble that went into making the manga, and also sorry...

I give words of thanks for everyone, as well as good luck!

With luck,
Temari Matsumoto